Don't take my grief away from me.

How to Walk Through Grief and Learn to Live Again

by

Doug Manning

Don't Take My Grief Away From Me
Doug Manning

Revised Edition ©2005

In-Sight Books, Inc
PO Box 42467
Oklahoma City, Oklahoma 73123
800.658.9262 or 405.810.9501
www.InSightBooks.com
OrdersAndInfo@InSightBooks.com

First Edition ©1979 by In-Sight Books, Inc.

Printed in the United States of America

ISBN 1-892785-04-8

In-Sight Books, Inc.
Since 1979 Helping People Help People

4/09

DEDICATION

To Anne and Jess Wade—
The night of their great loss gave birth to
this book.
This book is dedicated to them in the hope that
their honesty in grief can produce healing for all
who read it.

March 1, 1979

TABLE OF CONTENTS

Right now you do not feel like reading a book. All you feel is numbness and unreality.

For the next few days there will be very little time to read. You must make decisions. Family must be gathered in. A funeral must be planned.

For now, read the first section of the book. It will help you in the decisions you must make.

Read Section One and then lay the book aside. In a week or so pick it up again and let it help you walk through your grief and learn to live again.

SECTION I

THE FUNERAL

You probably have never had to plan a funeral. Suddenly you must do so. There must be a thousand questions you would like to ask if you knew what they were, and if you knew whom to ask.

This section of the book will not answer all of the questions, but it may help you answer some of them.

The following short chapters are here to help you get through the decision-making days.

If there are other questions on your mind, let loose and ask. There are answers. None of the questions you ask will be either silly or a bother.

You are not expected to be an expert on funerals. You are not expected to be calm and logical. You are not expected to be thinking straight. Feel free to ask any question you want to ask, feel free to ask whatever you want, and express whatever you feel.

*A*t first it feels as if there are
a thousand things to do and
you do not know how to do any of them.
You will learn how and be helped with
each step in the learning.

1.

WHERE DO I BEGIN?

One of the feelings usually felt by people in the first shock of grief is: "There must be a thousand things to do, but what are they?" This feeling hits you very soon after a death and seems to be overwhelming. You feel you should be doing something, but do not know what must be done, nor where to begin.

Relax—there is not all that much to do. There will be people available to help you with the things which must be done.

The Funeral Director: You can trust the funeral director to make most of the arrangements. You can trust him to remember the details. You can trust him to let you know any details for which you must be responsible.

The funeral director is a highly trained professional. His major contribution to you and your need is he has learned what needs to be done.

He knows what is proper and respectable. He knows a great deal about your needs in this time. He may seem to be a little too efficient for the occasion, but remember—someone needs to be efficient at this time.

Friends: Bless 'em—they are never more needed than right now. They seem to know what to do by instinct. They want to help. Some of them say the wrong things. Some may be overzealous in their efforts, but they are there because they love you.

There are many things friends can do for you right now.

They can help make the phone calls necessary to inform family and friends. Some of these calls you may want to make personally. If so, do not be afraid to say so. Sometimes a friend may dominate the situation just because you are afraid to speak up for fear of offending. Make it clear what you want to do and what you would like help in doing.

Friends can help in food preparation. One way they can let you know of their love and concern is by bringing food and helping in the kitchen. This releases you from a real burden.

Fortunately, there are some things you must do. This is fortunate because you need some things to do at this time. Your involvement in these things will give you a sense of sharing your love for the loved one who has passed away.

You will be involved in selecting the service, planning the funeral, choosing a place of burial—if this has not been previously arranged—choosing flowers for the casket, choosing pall bearers, and other details.

The funeral director will guide you in each of these decisions. He will remember them. He will tell you when each decision needs to be made. He will not make the decisions for you, but he will not let you leave out any of them.

The days ahead will be trying days. There really are not a thousand things to do. You will have ready help in everything that must be done. Don't panic at the thought of so much to do. Relax as best you can and trust the help you have to get it all done.

A funeral is your gift of love.
Make it your gift and give it in Freedom.

2.

CHOICES

How do you want the funeral to be done? That is the only question to be asked right now. What would please you?

There are many social customs which have become the regular pattern for funerals. These social customs can become a source of pressure on you. If you are not careful, these customs will force you to just go along when you may have strong feelings and desires to do things your own way.

Social customs or not, the funeral should fit you and your desires. You may have a fear of shocking your friends. You may find that most of your friends will not be shocked at all. Many of them have feelings about bucking the customs themselves, and the feelings to be considered are yours and those of the immediate family. Choose those persons in your family you want to help you plan how to memorialize your loved one in a manner that will comfort you. To avoid a time of conflict or arguing with family members who may object to your plans, quietly say, "This is how it is to be." Stand firm early in the arrangements, the family will usually hush. If they do not hush, continue to stand firm. This is one time you have the right to your way. The funeral should accomplish two things and only two things. First, it should memorialize your loved one. Second, it should comfort you. Whatever arrangements accomplish those two things are right. All else is secondary. That may sound harsh and selfish, but in reality, it is neither. To have people force their will upon you at this time is harsh and selfish. To have the right to arrange the funeral as you feel it should be is your God-given privilege. No one should take that away from you.

How do you want the funeral to be done? That question also applies in ways other than social custom and family. All through this book we will be fighting the presence of guilt. Right here is where the struggle with guilt must begin.

The immediate reaction to making funeral arrangements will be, "How would the person who has passed want it to be?" This can lead to utter frustration, for you probably do not know how that person would want it to be. You can only guess and hope you hit. Later you might think of things you forgot and feel guilty because of their omission.

Guilt can cause you to try to make up to the person for any slights by demonstrating love in the form of an expensive funeral. The result can be costly financially and totally unrewarding emotionally.

The perspective should be: I am now called upon to plan a fitting memorial to a life. I should plan this memorial as I think and feel it should be done. The planning and the memorial are my gifts to this life. It is my way of expressing how I feel and what the person meant to me. The funeral can fit this perspective if it is done as you and those you choose to be a part in the planning see it and feel it.

If done in an effort to follow how the person to be memorialized would want it, then it is not your gift to that person. It is just your following out some vague plan.

Most of the time there is no detailed plan to follow—only general assumptions with no real guidelines.

If done in some effort to make up to them, then it is not your gift. It is you making a futile attempt to struggle with guilt.

Plan a memorial as you think it should be, and let that planning be a gift of love to the one who has departed. Do it your way.

*The funeral is your
gift of Love.
How this gift is voiced
is part of the Gift.
Who voices the gift matters.
The voice must be your choice.*

3.

WHAT ABOUT A MINISTER?

Once again—how do you want the funeral to be done? That question should determine your choice of a minister. It should also determine your choice of whether or not a minister is used.

In many faiths the minister question will not even arise. There are faiths which have a definite ceremony for funerals, and the ceremony will be the same no matter which minister or priest performs the rites. If you have worshiped with these rites through the years, they have become very dear to you and will provide a meaningful experience of worship at the memorial service.

In other faiths the ceremony depends on the minister. In these faiths there will be a variance in the services as to types and messages. If you have a minister who has been close to you and your family through the years, do not hesitate to call for his services. If he can be present, he will be more comfort to you than any other minister.

I was a minister. I know families in my church often did not feel free to call another minister for fear of hurting my feelings. I wish this were not so. I wanted the family to have the person and the service they need at this time.

I remember a specific instance when, for fear of hurting me, a family would not call an old friend of theirs to officiate the service. I urged them to do so, but they did not take my urgings seriously, I knew how close this minister was to this family. He had lived in their home. He had performed the marriage of each of their children. I honestly wanted him to be there. I thought he could meet needs I could not come close to touching.

Even though he was not called, he came to the service. He slipped in the back just as the service began. It was too late for me to involve him in the service. As soon as the funeral was over I slipped to the back of the church and asked him to stand with me beside the coffin. When the family saw him as they were leaving the church they ran to him and were met with warm embraces.

I stood to the side and worshiped. Human love is very precious to me. To see it in action is one of the grandest sights in the world. The family noticed me standing to the side and began to try to reassure me of their love. They had no idea how glad I was to see the person who could give the most comfort be there and give it.

A funeral does not have to be religious. It is acceptable to have a funeral without the services of a clergy person. A good friend or family member can do a great job of making the funeral meaningful. There are now Certified Funeral Celebrants in many parts of the country who are specifically trained to provide beautiful personalized services. Your funeral director can tell you if there is a Celebrant available in your area.

By all means use the person who can mean the most to you. Remember, as an act of love you are preparing *your* memorial to a loved one. Whatever and whoever fits your plans for this memorial are right.

The first step toward recovering from grief may be the hardest step of all.
The first step is facing the reality of death.
No one can make that step an easy one.

4.

SHOULD I GO SEE THE BODY?

I sat in the waiting room of a funeral home holding the hands of a mother and her daughter. We were waiting for arrangements to be finished so we could see the body of their husband and father. Yesterday he had been among them. A car wreck meant today he was gone.

As we waited they were undecided as to whether or not they wanted to see the body. There was a strong desire to run away from the funeral home and not go through the ordeal. I urged them to stay. It may sound strange, or even cruel, for me to have urged hurting people to hurt even more by going through such an ordeal.

We walked into the view room together. The first shock was very hard. Gradually we were able to settle down and basically just stand there. Not much was said. The wife rearranged his hair so it would be more normal. The daughter hugged her mother—giving reassurance and receiving it at the same time.

We sat for awhile in the room. The wife finally spoke. She said, "It isn't real until you see it, is it? Until now it was all just a dream. Now I know it is real, and I must face it."

Viewing the body is one of the hardest, and yet one of the healthiest things done at funerals. The first step toward handling grief is to face the fact of death. This is tough and hurts, but it is one of the necessary hurts if you are to find healing.

Our society tries to avoid facing death. We would like to arrange nice funerals which hide the fact that someone has died. The result is often a long period of mental denial which leads to a much longer period of recovery. The answer is to grasp a new concept of death.

Years ago, on Easter, the *New York Times* carried a cartoon on the front page showing a group of caterpillars carrying a cocoon to the cemetery. They were dressed all in black and were in deep mourning. Up in the top of the drawing was a beautiful butterfly. The caption read, "What the caterpillar calls the end, God calls a butterfly." I hope you can discover the butterfly in the days ahead.

Should you go view the body? Again, it is your choice. I am not trying to force or even convince you as to what you should do. I want you to see the reasons for doing so and then to decide for yourself. I am prejudiced, and that prejudice shows, but it does not mean I am right. Nor does it mean what I have said applies in all cases.

There are those who think the preparation of the body for viewing is plastic. There are those who think the viewing of the bodies is a pagan rite and comes close to worshiping the body.

I do not think either is true. Folks say they want to remember them as they were. The trouble is those of us close to the person may have had a very unpleasant last view to remember.

I was with my grandfather when he died. I had never seen death before. I remember how he looked that night. My last memory of him is how he looked in the casket after he had been prepared. I treasure that last memory and last look. I am glad my last look was not the night I held his hand while he died.

The other problem with remembering them as they were is that it can become a dreamy state for you. The person is gone on a trip and not here now. You may not fully realize that the person is dead; and you must adjust to this fact.

I know it is hard, but I do think the family should see the body. There should never be pressure nor rejection involved. If one does not want to go—let him read this chapter and decide for himself.

I do not know how much value there is to other people viewing the body. Whether this is done at the funeral home or at the service is a matter of personal preference. I have officiated at many funerals, and of course, have had many where the body was placed for viewing and many where it was not. I have not noticed any appreciable difference in the effect on the family or the service.

Public viewing of the body is purely a matter of personal taste and preference. Do it your way.

I feel like I have said, "Do it your way," and then tried to talk you into my way. I do have strong feelings in this area. I do so because of experience and study. I want to walk you through grief. I know that the first step is facing the reality of death. Viewing the body can be a help in this area.

A funeral director friend of mine lost a son in a plane crash. After the crash the family received an urn with the ashes said to be those of their son. My friend is a highly trained professional mortician. He is certainly accustomed to death and knows the process of recovery. He now says the process was made much more difficult because he could not grasp the reality of the situation. He had fantasies about the ashes not being those of his son, and that his son was not dead. Maybe his son escaped the crash and was lost in the woods near the crash site. Maybe he was not on the plane. The reality was delayed because the body was not there to force the facing of death.

This is why I have been too persuasive in this chapter. I want you well. I honestly think this is a step forward to being well again.

Flowers say I love you
    and I am with you in your
sorrow.
In grief we need someone to say
    I love you,
    I am with you,
    I care.
Let them say it again and again.

5.

WHAT DO FLOWERS MEAN?

Until a few years ago there was no question about flowers at a funeral. It was the accepted custom for folks to send flowers. Somewhere along the way it became the "in thing" to ask that donations be made to a charity instead. The idea behind this is that the flowers are a waste. They will not last very long, and the money is just thrown away. Why not let the money be spent where it will do some good?

The problem with this idea is that the flowers do good, even if they do not last long. I have interviewed several people about what they remember about the funeral of a loved one and what had meaning to them. Flowers were high on the list of memories and meaning of every person I have spoken to.

When my grandmother died I was in deep grief. She was a very special person in my life. I do not remember anything about the service except the flowers. I was overwhelmed by their number and their beauty. I remember looking at them and realizing they meant she was loved by many people. I remember thinking that I, too, must be loved by many people, for many flowers were sent by friends of my family who did not know my grandmother. Somehow the flowers gave significance to her life and to mine.

When my father-in-law died, a friend in the city where I lived wired flowers to the city where my father-in-law lived. He was thoughtful enough to do this early enough to be

20

sure the flowers were in the viewing room the first time the family went in to see the body. I cannot begin to tell you what this meant to me and to the family. The friend who did this is a funeral director in my city. He knew the value of flowers, and he shared with us in our time of need.

In grief we need people. Flowers can be with us when friends cannot be present. Flowers can say words friends may not be able to express. I will give to charity on my own at other times. When someone is in grief I try to go be with them, and I send flowers to be with them. When I am in grief, I need to be given to. I am a "charity" in this case. I am in need. To deny my friends the privilege to help me in my need is to rob both of us.

Several people I have interviewed told of using the potted plants brought to the home as a means of expressing thanks. After the funeral they took some of these to the friends who had been a help to them during their grief.

I may be old-fashioned and not with the times, but I think the idea of flowers being sent is beautiful and healthy. Allow yourself to be ministered to in this way. It will be a help to you and a blessing to the friend who sends them.

Flowers don't last very long and are a waste? The memory of the flowers at my grandmother's funeral has remained fresh in my mind for over forty years. Their meaning is still fresh even though the flowers are gone. Anything that can have meaning for this length of time cannot be a waste.

Children feel, even if they do not understand. Understanding comes later— the feelings need a hug.

6.

THE CHILDREN

If you have young children you have a decision to make. How much should they be told? How involved should they be in the funeral? How do they express grief? How can you help them in this struggle?

The answers depend on the age of the child. There are no hard and fast rules—no matter what the age of the child. The individual child must be considered in relation to his/her sensitivity, and relationship to the person who has passed away.

Some general ideas are:

Under two years of age, children will have no understanding of death, but will have some general feeling that something is wrong. Even at this age children sense when parents are upset. It is important that children not be forgotten in the chaos of this period. They will need attention and love. They will need to be held and touched. If your children are sent to be with friends or family, take care to be sure you have time with them throughout this period.

Children aged three-to-five will have some sense of there having been a bad event. They will not understand death to any degree of depth. They will sense the general upset around them and have feelings of insecurity. Again, take care to be sure the children are touched and loved. If they ask questions, answer them as calmly and simply as possible. They may ask what death means. If your children have had any experience with death through the loss of a pet, it could be the answer would simply be, "It is like when the goldfish died. There comes a time when things die." No long explanation is needed, but to just brush aside the question with "You are too young to understand," can add to the children's sense of insecurity.

Children aged six-to-eight will be very similar except at this age children are more likely to ask questions. Answer the questions calmly and honestly. If possible, have a private moment with your child to give the chance for questions. Children of this age should not be shuttled off away from the family and left out. They, too, will grasp the feelings of insecurity and often are left to make their own conclusions about the event. Often these conclusions are wrong and can color their thinking and feelings in the years ahead.

Children aged nine-to-twelve years will understand the event to a surprising degree. They will relate to the event in their own terms. They probably will talk about the race car they were building and now cannot finish—or the trip they now will not get to take. At first this may seem to be selfish on their part. It is not selfish at all. It is their way of expressing the loss they feel in the terms of the world they are in. Instead of rejecting the children's terms, get in there with them. Let them talk out their loss in whatever terms they feel. Children of this age should not be left out of the overall funeral process. To leave them out may seem protective; instead of protecting, it can create feelings of rejection and insecurity. They, too, must learn to deal with the loss. Children need the family to help them in this process.

Children aged thirteen-to-sixteen are at a difficult age. Feelings, thoughts, emotions, and physical growth are all trying to develop at the same time. It is difficult for all of these to line up in proper order. It is very easy for children of this age to connect the event to their own feelings and thus create guilt. If they have done some wrong in the recent past, children may decide the death happened as punishment to them. They will not know how to express these feelings and will probably not try to do so. It may be some time after the event before children are ready to talk, but at some point you need to be sensitive enough to pick up on their clues and hear them out.

The clues may be silent. Children may begin to spend more time alone. The clues may be rebellion or lashing out. The clues may be little hints. You need to be aware of the fact that your children may be having a struggle and may need to talk.

This need to talk is especially true if the one lost is a member of the immediate family. The loss of a father, mother, brother, or sister will mean children of this age must deal with grief and loss. They should not be pried open, of course. In a private time or in several private times, talk out the subject with openness and honesty. Deal with all questions. Allow feelings. To tell children they should not think the way they are thinking comes across as an attack. It is much better to say "I can understand why you feel this way—do you want to talk about it?"

There are no magic formulas to work in dealing with children and death. In this case, love and good ears are the major needs and the best medicine. If children know you love them and know you will listen, you can help them through grief no matter how untrained and unprepared you feel.

The major things to help them avoid are:

Insecurity during the time of the funeral process...
This process includes the days of preparation when the house is full of people and general chaos is the order of the day, as well as the funeral itself.

Guilt, which can be real or imagined...
You will have to fight the "If I had only" in your own grief—so will the children.

Rejection, which can happen by the child just getting lost in the crowd and no one noticing...
In this "lostness" they can come to conclusions which are hard to overcome.

Right now all you feel is *your* needs. That is normal and right. It is not selfishness on your part. It is the strong drive of self-survival. It will take all the strength you can muster to even think of the children right now. At times it will be impossible to do so. Others can help with this task right now. Let them do so. In the days ahead you will be able to give of yourself more and more. There will be time to do so. All you need now is to be aware and give what you can. It cannot be done in a day. Just get through this hard part without rejecting the children. In the days ahead you can help each other in the grief process.

The family—
I need them,
They need me,
We need each other
so
desperately.

7.

THE FAMILY TIME

Friends are wonderful. In time of grief they are not only wonderful—they are absolutely essential. People need people to help them in grief. It may sound religious to say "All I need is God." It is neither religious nor true. Prayer is great in grief, but nothing takes the place of a warm person being with you in your pain.

Some friends will be much more help than others. Some will be overzealous and take over. Some will be far too quick to give advice and philosophy. Some will say the wrong things. The friends who quietly stand with you and hold your hand will overcome any problems caused by those who just do not know what to do when someone hurts.

With all that good friends do and all the help they give, they can create some problems without ever meaning to do so. They need to be there, but the very fact that they are there means you must do all of your grieving in public. You will go through day after day of telling your story, or at least trying to do so, to each new friend or relative who arrives. Usually you will get the story half told and there will be another to arrive. You will stop the story, greet the new arrival, and start telling it all over again.

This means you will have very little time to gather together your thoughts and feelings. You will be in a constant state of greeting people and trying to complete all of the details of funeral arrangements. There will be so many interruptions that there will be no time for you to be alone to think through the event.

This process also means there will be no time for you and your immediate family to be together. At the time when the family needs each other the most, it will be almost impossible to find the time and solitude to give each other.

The result will be, the things which need to be said, the feelings which need to be expressed, and the memories which need to be shared among the family can be lost in the shuffle of folks.

When my father-in-law died I experienced this effect to its fullest. There are two ministers in my wife's family, and neither of us wanted to take over for fear of offending the other. I knew we needed a time for just us, but I did nothing to create the situation. We went through the days and were never alone together as a family. A day or so after the funeral I drove home alone. There were so many things inside of me I wanted to express I thought I would pop. I wanted to tell my mother-in-law how much I loved her. I wanted to tell the whole family how much my father-in-law had meant to me. I longed to share with them the experiences and memories I held dear. I wanted to hear from the family their experiences and memories. As I drove home I ached because I knew there would never be the time to get together in this setting and share. In all the years that have passed; we have not had the chance again.

When my wife returned home there seemed to be a barrier between us. For days we carried on as if nothing had happened. Neither of us wanted to bring up the subject. It is hard to tell another how much you hurt unless you know how much he/she hurts. I was afraid to say anything for fear of upsetting my wife. She was afraid to bring it up for fear I did not share the same hurts, and she would seem foolish. One night I could stand it no longer, I told her how much I was hurting, I told her I was lying awake at night with the awful reality that I would never see her father again, Thank goodness I did so, for the dam broke and the barriers came down. We began to deal with the other's grief and to help one another.

These barriers are very real in a family's grief. They need to be broken down as a group. My wife and I were able to break through ours. We have not been able to do so with the rest of the family. I have no idea how the other children in the family and their children feel. We go on as if nothing has happened.

Something needs to happen with just the immediate family during the days of the funeral experience to break down these barriers and begin the process of communication.

For several years I have been organizing an event to meet this need. I call it the family time. The night before the funeral I ask for an hour with the family in a setting that gives complete privacy. We may go to my office. We may go to a friend's house. We may go to the funeral home. The setting does not matter. The time together without interruption does matter.

Often when I first mention such a time together the family is a little reluctant. They are afraid the meeting will be sad and morbid. It never is that way at all. We just sit down together and begin to talk about who the person was and what he/she meant to us. Someone remembers a story; this causes someone else to remember another event. The family has a time together to start the flow of memory, and to share the significance of a life.

This is a wonderful time for the children. They can share their feelings. They can hear the stories and experiences. They can grasp the value of the person who has died. I have seen these events bring alienated and rebellious young people into a closer relationship with the family.

A private time together is good even if there has been friction in the family. If there is anger it needs to be expressed. One of the best family times I have ever witnessed was one in which there was anger. One son-in-law who had had a great deal of struggle with his father-in-law was able to say so in openness and honesty. He finally was able to say, "You know he and I both are bullheaded, but I think we really loved each other."

The night before my grandmother's funeral my father said, "Let's go down and visit Momma Hoyle." We went to the funeral home, sat by her casket, and swapped yarns for hours. I do not remember the funeral the next day, but I shall never forget the night when we visited together about who she was and what she meant to us.

The family time is much like the traditional Irish wake. When people talk about the Irish Wake they often remark about the drinking that sometimes happens there, but the wakes are more than a party or a time for drinking. The people get together to talk about the person who has been among them. The family needs a time like this.

There are several ways to set up this time. You may ask your pastor or Celebrant to help you do so. Ask him/her to read this chapter and then lead in the experience.

You may just go to the funeral home for a visit together and have the experience happen spontaneously. Or you may ask some person in the immediate family to take charge of organizing the time and place for this event.

It will not be easy. To have a family time will mean telling some people who are coming to call that you will be gone for an hour. People will understand and certainly can wait in your home. There will be others in your home with whom they can visit.

It may even mean leaving some relatives at home, and initially they may not understand. This time is important enough to risk hurting some feelings. Just tell others you need a time with the immediate family, and that this is the only time you will have. Let them read this chapter—maybe it will explain your need to them.

This time needs to be before the funeral. After the funeral some of the family will be leaving. Other relatives will need to be told goodbye. The need to settle business matters while the family is together will dominate the time after the funeral. The barriers will have already been put up. The event will be over, and everyone will seem to think and to feel the less said, the better.

As I said, most families approach this event with some reluctance. Almost without fail they later tell me it was the most meaningful thing they can remember doing. Try a time together.

The funeral is your gift of Love.
It is a celebration of
the Life,
the Death,
and the Hope
of a meaningful person.
Share the meaning.

8.

MAKE IT PERSONAL

For some reason our society has decided a person should not be eulogized. Families tell me they do not want me to brag on the person. Ministers tell me they want to tell about the person, but feel they are doing wrong and should not be giving glory to a human being.

The result is that most funerals could fit everyone. General statements are made about life and death. Impersonal philosophies are shared, and almost nothing is said about the unique person who has passed from us.

If I understand the Bible, persons give glory to God. He made us and is proud of what He made. Whatever we have become gives glory to Him. I think we pay the ultimate homage to God when we celebrate the life of one of His creations.

If I understand the need of people in grief, they need to feel the significance of the life lived among them.

Therefore, a funeral should be a very personal celebration of the life, love, death, and hope of the person.

Do not be afraid to request such a service. If your minister is not prone to such a service, or if your faith does not provide for individualized funerals, then ask a friend or a Certified Celebrant to deliver a eulogy.

One of the most meaningful funerals I have ever experienced had a statement of love read by a son-in-law of the man who had died. The whole family worked on the statement. In the private family time they discussed the things to be included. It was read with dignity and love. Nothing I might have said could have meant as much to the family as this beautiful expression of love.

In the most effective funeral I have ever officiated I said nothing. I was called to perform a graveside rite for the grandfather of a counseling client. I knew no one there except the granddaughter. I simply said I did not know the man, but they did know him. I asked that they express what he had meant to them. Almost everyone spoke. The experience was not morbid, nor was it overly sentimental. They memorialized the life in a way I could never begin to duplicate. In the beauty of the event, I closed in prayer.

There is nothing wrong with the funeral being personal. There is almost everything right with it being so. The message, the music, the words of remembrance, and the style should fit the person. Feel free to let it do so.

I believe in eternal life. I believe we live on after this life is over—in a new and better life beyond death. I believe we also live on in the lives of those we have touched.

They say my grandmother died in 1960. They are wrong. Each time the family gets together we swap yarns about her. I know the yarns by heart. I even know the order in which they will be told. I love to hear those stories. This is the way she lives on. Hardly a week goes by but that I think of her. A family gathering never happens but that she comes to life among us. My children know her well even though she died before they were old enough to remember. She lives on in us. She can never die as long as we live.

This is the way your loved one will live on also. The private family time can begin the process of such living on. The funeral, too, should be a beginning of this process.

They will never die as long as you live—for we live on in a new world and in the lives of those we have touched.

I am sure you have found it difficult to read this much of the book.
Time has been hard to come by.
Your mind has not wanted to focus.
Your shock has been too great.

The second part of the book is for later.
In it I will try to walk with you through your grief.
I will try to help you live again.

But it is for reading a little later. Lay the book aside for now. After the folks have gone home and you feel ready, pick up the book and begin the process of learning to live again.

SECTION II

UNDERSTANDING DEATH

*R*ight now your chest hurts—
   The numbness has worn off and real pain
      has replaced it.
   You wonder if you will ever be well again.
   A thousand questions flood your mind.
   A thousand hurts pop up every day—
Every day you find a new thing to cause memories and
      bring tears.
   You find it hard to sleep.
   The awful loneliness seems to be there every moment of
      every day.
   The finality of death leaves a hollow feeling all over
      your body.
Loneliness comes in only one size—Extra Large.
   Maybe through this book I can help—I hope it
      becomes a friend you turn to again and again in
      the days ahead.
I wrote the book trying to be a friend.
   If it helps you it must accomplish at least two things.
   It must help you to develop a healthy concept of death,
      and
   It must help you to walk through the process of grief
      and learn to live again.
Shall we try?

Wouldn't it be just like God to make even death a Pleasant Experience?

9.

WHAT HAPPENS WHEN SOMEONE DIES?

She was a delightful lady of seventy-six years. A broken ankle meant she had to have what was thought to be a very simple surgery procedure. She was to have a pin placed into the bone of her ankle. No one was particularly concerned about the surgery. The procedure went well, and all signs pointed to a routine recovery.

When the surgery was over and the patient was awakening in the recovery room, her heart suddenly stopped. No warning—no reason—her heart just stopped. The surgical team reacted quickly and efficiently, and in a matter of moments her heart responded, and the crisis passed.

The next evening I visited her in the hospital. I was totally unprepared for the experience we had together. When I walked into the room she immediately began to relate her experience. She said:

> "Pastor, I am so glad you are here. I want to tell my story to someone, but every time I try no one will listen or understand. When I tell my family, they think I am crazy or morbid, or want to die. None of this is true.
>
> "I am old and do not have a great deal to live for, but I am not morbid, nor crazy, nor do I want to die.
>
> "I have been giving a great deal of thought to the word 'death'…the act of dying. You see, my heart

stopped yesterday. I want you to know what I felt during that period. I was out of my body. I was up on the ceiling looking back on all the things going on. I could see the doctors working on my body, but I was not there.

"Pastor, I felt wonderful. I cannot describe it to you except to say it was the most wonderful feeling of well-being I have ever known. I felt if they would just turn me loose and let me go on, everything would be all right. And I fought them. I am ashamed to say that, but I fought the doctors. I wanted them to get their hands off me and not to take this feeling away from me.

"Then I was back in my body.

"Now, I am not morbid or wishing for death, but I feel they cheated me out of my trip. Do you understand what I mean by that?"

I held her hand and said:

"Do you know what you are telling me? You are telling me that death itself is a pleasant experience. We have feared it for all of our lives. For centuries people have feared it. But wouldn't it be just like God to make even death a pleasant experience?

"The Bible says, 'Death, where is thy sting?' I have always looked at that statement from a theological stance. Your experience makes me look at it from a whole different perspective. Death has no sting because it is a pleasant experience. I never thought I would ever say this to anyone, but I am sorry you did not get to make the trip."

She said, "Thank you—you understand."

I could not escape this experience. It caused me to want to know more about the word "death"...more about "the act of dying."

Much research about death has been done in the last few years. This research has proven the experience of my friend to be true. Elisabeth Kubler-Ross, a brilliant psychological researcher, did massive studies in the field of death and dying. Others have followed in her pioneering steps. Many books have been written documenting the research.

The result is that we now have the basis for believing that what this lady friend of mine experienced is the way death happens.

Interviews with thousands of people who have suffered momentary death and have been brought back all confirm the same experience. It is remarkable how their stories agree in almost every detail.

There is a buzzing sound. It is not unpleasant
or unbearable—
There is a sense of being out of the body watching
the event take place—
There is a sense of total awareness of all the things being
said or done while the event is in progress—
There is an overwhelming feeling of well-being—
There is a reluctance to return—

There is usually the meeting of someone who has
already died. A loved one, the Virgin Mary,
or even Jesus Christ—
There is a lack of fear
And after the event is over, the person has a new perspective about death.

I believe this is what happened to your loved one. No
matter the circumstances of the death, the event itself was
the pleasant passage to a new adventure.

You may have had an experience in the last few weeks
when it seemed as if the person was there with you. It may
have been an almost physical thing when you felt the presence as real as life itself. It may be just some clue that seems
to say to you that the person has been near. Many people experience such an event. Most are afraid to report it because
they think no one will understand. Some are even afraid
they are crazy. This experience is a fairly common occur-
rence, and you are not crazy. There are many things we do
not know about life beyond. Who can say there is not a
chance for a loved one to come by just to say good-bye?

All of the research at least proves one thing to us: death
is not the end—it is the beginning.

Your loved one has begun—

*Eternity will have to last a
Long time—
I have enough questions
to fill up a thousand years.*

10.

WHY?

You have the right to ask why—you will ask it whether or not you are given the right.

Some folks will be very quick to say you are not to ask why—you are merely to accept.

Others will be ready with all kinds of philosophic answers to why this happened.

Others will fill the air with theological answers which may help them, but somehow do not do much for you at this point.

No one knows why—I am guilty of trying to answer the question with trite statements myself. I say, "If bad things happened only to bad people, we would all be good for the wrong reasons." That sounds good, but does not do much to answer the question.

A friend of mine lost a child to leukemia. He reported that there seemed to be some dead ends in trying to face the "why" in such a tragic event. He said the first dead end is the idea that it can be understood. The second dead end is the idea that we are not even supposed to question. We are to be stoical and just take it.

In the midst of his struggle a letter came from a friend. All the letter said was, "John, God's got a lot to give an account for." At first my friend was shocked at this statement. It seemed blasphemous. The longer he thought about it, the more sense it made. God does have a lot to give an account for. Maybe faith is not knowing the answer to the why. Maybe faith is being willing to wait for the answer. Maybe faith is knowing there will be a time when it will be explained; that we will not be treated as a thing to which events happen with no explanation forthcoming. We shall, rather, be dealt with as persons who deserve an explanation and will one day receive it.

By the way, the friend in question is John Claypool. He has written the account of his loss in a beautiful book called *Tracks of a Fellow Struggler: Living and Growing through Grief.** I recommend that you read this book. The chapter called "Life is Gift" just happens to be one of the best things ever written.

The answer to the why may not come in our lifetime. There is just too much of the beyond we cannot grasp right now. The living without an answer is not easy. I am not sure it is made any easier by the idea that one day we will have an answer. To be truthful, we want it now.

Living without the answer will mean you may go through some reactions. It makes grief recovery a great deal harder. Having no answer may make you angry with God. It may make you angry with life. It may cause you to feel cheated and unfairly persecuted.

The best thing I can say is to feel what you feel. The danger is that you will decide you should not have such feelings and that you are, therefore, either bad or crazy.

The truth is that these feelings will be there. To bury them does not cause them to go away. To deny them does not mean they are not there. The feelings will be there—so let them be there.

* John Claypool, *Tracks of a Fellow Struggler* (Harrisburg, PA: Morehouse Publishing, 2004), 45. ISBN 0-8192-2139-2

Hopefully, you have one friend with whom you can share. Hopefully, this friend will not react to what you feel by saying you should not feel the way you do. If you have such a friend, share how you feel. If you do not have such a friend, write out what you feel.

A terrible thing has happened. To make the event even worse there is no explanation as to why the event happened. What are you supposed to feel? Happiness? Joy? Thankfulness? How are you supposed to react? With a great burst of faith? With a carrying on as if nothing has happened?

No—you have been deeply hurt. You should, therefore, hurt deeply.

One day you will feel better.

One day you will live again.

Right now you are wounded—no explanation in the world will make that wound go away.

You have a thousand whys—ask them all.

You have a million feelings—feel them all.

You have a billion hurts—and you deserve every one of them.

For now, feel what you feel. Later you can deal with recovery. Right now all I want is to free you up to allow yourself the feelings that are there.

If no one can answer the why—then right now it just hurts.

*The best thing about
the other side of death is
there is no guilt there.
If there is none there, why
should there be any here?*

11.

IF ONLY—

The most natural reaction in the world is to look for someone or something to blame when a hurt is present.

You might fix the blame on the doctor or the hospital—or even on the person who died. Somehow the blame has to be transferred somewhere.

As most people do, you probably have transferred the blame to yourself.

"If only I had," becomes the beginning phrase of most of your sentences.

If only I had been there.

If only I had forced him to go to the doctor.

If only I had been a better husband.

If only I had been a better wife.

If only I had been a better father.

If only I had been a better mother.

If you are not careful, you may very quickly begin to fix guilt on yourself. If no guilt is there, you may manufacture some.

It may be that you feel the need to punish yourself.

It may be that you feel hurt and anger. Hurt or anger always needs some place to fixate. You do not know where else to put it, so you put it on yourself.

A young girl came to see me. Her story was one of the deeper tragedies I have ever dealt with. Her father had shot and killed her mother. In one horrible moment she had lost her mother by death and her father by the horror of his deed. You can imagine the feelings which ran through her mind and heart.

When tragedy strikes feelings run rampant. These feelings ultimately become anger. You may not recognize them as anger because you think of anger as being mad or being out of control. Anger can also be hurt. Anger can also be frustration. Call it whatever you wish—the feelings are the same and the results are the same. When these feelings become anger or hurt or frustration, you seek someone to blame.

Where was my little friend going to place her feelings? She desperately fought to keep from feeling any stronger anger against her father than she already felt. She needed him now more than ever. He could not be with her, of course, but he was all she had. She was going to have a terrible time forgiving him or loving him without adding all of the anger and hurt to the relationship.

She shifted the blame to herself. She built up an elaborate fantasy in her mind. If she had gone to get her mother from work, her father would not have been there to meet her mother, and this would not have happened. If she had not overslept, she might have gone to get her mother. The whole thing happened because she overslept.

She had enough "if onlys" to last a lifetime. She had enough to make that lifetime miserable.

Are you at this point? Have you built up some "if onlys?"

If so, you need to think it through very carefully. Most of the "if onlys" are not really true.

Even the ones that are true are beyond your control. There is nothing you can do to change them.

What is happening to you is the same thing my little friend experienced. The hurt and anger you feel inside need a place to fix the blame. You have elected yourself to be that place.

It will be much better if you can admit to yourself that you are angry, that you have feelings of hurt. You should have these feelings. There is no need to fix the blame. There is no need to punish yourself. There is no need to deny your feelings.

It helps a great deal to sort out the feelings and admit they are there. Instead of playing "what if," say, "I am hurt," or "I am angry." No blame—no guilt—just, something happened to me, and this is how I feel.

If the "what ifs" are not handled, they can grow into reactions. You can begin to punish yourself with these feelings until you become your own worst enemy.

I have known people who sentenced themselves to years of suffering as payment for these feelings. One man who lost two children by drowning became an alcoholic because of the guilt he felt over not teaching his children to swim. For thirteen years he locked himself off from the world. He divorced his wife, would never talk of the children, would never go to the cemetery, and would never deal with his feelings. He thought he deserved to suffer, and suffer he did.

I know a lady who has become a hermit; a prisoner in her own home. She has unresolved feelings of guilt because she did not force her husband to go to the doctor when he showed signs of heart disease. She has sentenced herself to loneliness to pay for her failure.

54

I know others who spend the rest of their lives making the person who died into a saint. The person who died becomes larger than life—they become the perfect mate. All the person can talk about is how wonderful the one who has died was when he/she was alive. Often this is a guilt reaction. It can be an effort to make up to the person for some slights, either real or imagined.

It is much healthier to deal with the feelings you have. You are not to blame. You were not the perfect mate, father, mother, brother, sister, but neither is anyone else.

If death is what it seems to be, and if life beyond is what it seems to be, your loved one has begun a new adventure. How could that person feel resentment toward you? How could he or she feel cheated? How could he/she want you punished? He/she is in a new adventure far greater than yours. You did not cheat the person—nor cause him/her to miss life. There is no guilt on that side of death—why should there be guilt on this side?

SECTION III

GRIEF

If I could do what I wanted to do for you right now, I would make you feel normal.

I would hold your hand as you told me of the feelings you are having inside, and I would say—

Yes, that is how it feels to be in grief.

Yes, that is a normal reaction.

Yes, as you progress through grief you have thoughts like that.

I cannot be there to hold your hand and say yes. I hope this book will be a substitute—I hope it will let you know you are normal.

Grief is bad enough. To experience it and not know what to expect or how you should feel makes the experience worse—much worse.

Read on and learn to feel normal.

Grieving is as natural as crying when you are hurt, sleeping when you are tired, eating when you are hungry, or sneezing when your nose itches. It is nature's way of healing a broken heart.

12.

DON'T TAKE MY GRIEF AWAY FROM ME

I have always thought she was *brilliance under pressure.* Her statement was a flash of insight in a time of darkness—a flash of insight which had a profound impact upon me.

Her little girl had the croup. Nothing seemed serious or unusual about it. Eighteen month old children can be sick enough to scare parents to death and two hours later they seem totally well. The croup worsened and the child was admitted to the hospital. Still there was no cause for fear. An oxygen tent, a vaporizer, some antibiotics and all would be well. The husband went home to care for the other child. In thirty minutes the child was dead. Just dead. This beautiful, effervescent life was gone.

Of all times for me to be 700 miles away on vacation, I had to pick this time. These were dear friends. Over the years they have become even dearer. In their hour of deepest need, I was away. As little as I knew about grief then, I probably would not have been much help had I been there. I would have felt better, but I am not sure this couple would have been helped very much by my presence or my philosophical answers.

The young mother was crying hysterically. It is strange that we cannot allow tears. Nothing is more natural than to cry. Nothing gets as quick a reaction from us as someone crying out of control. Everyone there that night began to react:

61

"There, there—now get hold of yourself."

"You can't carry on like this."

"Come on now—stop crying."

Suddenly the brave young mother looked them all in the eye. With fire in her voice she said:

"Don't take by grief from me. I deserve it. I am going to have it."

I did not hear her make the statement, and yet her words have haunted me for years. Her words have also done more to change my concept of grief and recovery than any words I have every heard.

I wondered how many times I had tried to take grief away from folks. How many times I had denied them the right to grieve in my presence because I made it quite clear I would not accept such activity.

I wondered how many times I had filled the air with philosophical statements to make it clear there would be no grief in my presence—statements designed to reassure *me* and to explain away tragedy far more than they were designed to help the person in grief.

I wondered how many times I had succumbed to the idea that sympathy was somehow harmful. It was almost as if I believed that if sympathy were given folks would wallow in it and never get well. These feelings seemed to be my stance. I do not know how I got around Jesus' standing at the tomb of a friend and weeping.

I wondered how many times I had taken away grief by sheer neglect. When the funeral was over, my work was done. I might have been a little more attentive the next time the person came to church—but beyond that, I went on as if nothing had happened. Most of the time they did go on as if nothing had happened, while inside they wept.

I wondered how many times I had taken away a person's grief by my efforts to avoid the intimacy and feelings I was forced to face in the process.

A young minister and his wife lost a child in a car wreck. They had many friends closer to them than my wife and I, yet they seemed drawn to our house. They came by night after night. When I dropped by their house they seemed relieved and pleased. One night they told us the reason. We were the only ones willing to talk about their child. We called her by name and seemed to have no feeling of being uncomfortable in doing so. Everyone else seemed to take great pains in avoiding the subject. If the child was mentioned, the subject was changed abruptly. When they told us we were different I breathed a sigh of relief and prayer. I had stopped trying to take away grief and had begun helping people walk through it.

I also thought back to all of the times I had seen others try to take away grief. I still watch it happen and cringe at the sight of it.

People will try to take grief away from you also. They will not intend to do so, nor even realize they are doing so. You may not realize this is being done to you, but the effort will be there. The effort is subtle but very effective.

It is done by too many words. It is as though people think they have to defend God in grief. As soon as tragedy comes, people tend to crank up an inexhaustible supply of philosophical statements trying to explain it all. I guess they feel if they can explain it, the grief will go away.

When the young preacher lost a child, there were two statements I particularly remember. There were the usual ones of course, like "Ours is not to question why," and, "The Lord giveth and the Lord taketh away." But two seemed to me to be especially bad:

One person said, "We do not know what kind of person your little girl would have grown up to be. Maybe God knew and took her on before she had a chance to become bad."

Who wants to think their daughter would have been bad? That defends God, if He needs defense, but it defends Him at the cost of people He loves.

The other statement was made to me. Thank goodness it was not made to the couple. At least I hope it was not. The child died in a car wreck that also left the couple seriously injured. Another pastor and I sat up all night keeping vigil over our friends. Late in the night the pastor said:

"My church and the church this man pastors were having an attendance contest. Do you suppose God was not pleased with our contest and caused this to happen?"

I reacted far too strongly to a man who was honestly questioning. He, too, was in grief and searching for answers, and I was not sensitive to him at all. All I felt was anger at the very idea and at what I considered to be a gross misunderstanding of God.

There are no philosophical answers to explain the tragedies of life. No one can understand why tragedies are there, much less explain them. Why must we try? There are no explanations and even if there were, explanations do not heal.

It is done by neglect—by avoiding the subject. By expecting folks to carry on as if nothing had happened. People do not actually say it, but they often leave the impression that if grief lingers, it is a sign of weakness in a person or in their faith. You tend to feel under pressure to recover quickly to prove your mental strength or your faith. I hear accounts of folks giving testimonies in church about how they have won the victory over grief only weeks after a loss. I hear of these and feel sad. In almost every case the person has not felt free to grieve. To not feel free means there must be a denial of grief. To deny means it must be swallowed. To swallow grief means you are going to be sick. Swallowed feelings do not go away. They surface as illness, nervousness, tension, and depression.

It is done by reacting. There are stages of grief which must be walked through. You can deny the stages and fake recovery, but the stages are still there. The stages produce symptoms which also must be walked through.

The problem is that very few people understand the stages or the symptoms. Not understanding often results in their reacting to you with "You ought not to feel like this." Or "You can't think this way."

Such reactions from others leave you wondering if you are weak or even crazy. The doubt causes you to redouble your efforts to not feel what you feel or at least not to show it. When you begin to make this effort your grief has been taken away from you.

Don't let anyone take your grief away from you. You deserve it and you must have it. If you had broken a leg, no one would criticize you for using crutches until it was healed. If you had major surgery, no one would pressure you to run in a marathon the next week. Grief is a major wound. It does not heal overnight. You must have the time and the crutches until you heal.

No one knows how long this should take. There is no timetable. You will heal in your own way and on your own timetable. To get over grief in a hurry does not mean you are superior. To take a long time does not mean you are weak. Quick recovery does not mean you did not love. Long recovery does not mean you did love. You will react to grief and recover from grief just like you react to all other things in life.

Recovery may take a couple of years—it may take much longer. There is no set timetable for healing to happen.

The problem will not only be that people may not give you the time to heal. The problem will also be that *you* may not give *yourself* the time needed. *You* may be the greatest source of pressure. It may be *you* who feels your faith is not strong if you are not well in a period of weeks. It may be *you* who tries to take your grief away.

You must give yourself permission to grieve. You are going to grieve whether or not you give yourself permission to do so. The difference is that if you do not give yourself permission, you will be in a state of war with yourself during the grieving process. If you do give yourself permission, you can relax and not fight against yourself or the process.

To fight against yourself is to add tension and hurt to the grief. To fight against yourself takes away energy desperately needed in grief recovery. To fight against yourself can lead you to *act* well long before you *are well*. Your act is just an act. It is not being well—it is only *acting* well. By acting you will lengthen the grief process. You may, as a result, have a relapse later when the acting well gets too much to bear.

You give yourself permission to grieve by recognizing the need for grieving. Grieving is the natural way of working through the loss of a love. Grieving is not weakness or absence of faith. Grieving is as natural as crying when you are hurt, sleeping when you are tired, or sneezing when your nose itches. It is nature's way of healing a broken heart.

Grief is not an enemy—it is a friend. It is the natural process of walking through hurt and growing because of the walk. Let it happen. Stand up tall to friends and to yourself and say, "Don't take my grief away from me. I deserve it and I am going to have it."

A cut finger—
is numb before it bleeds,
it bleeds before it hurts,
it hurts until it begins to heal,
it forms a scab and itches until
finally, the scab is gone and
a small scar is left where
once there was a wound.
Grief is the deepest wound you have
ever had. Like a cut finger,
it goes through stages and
leaves a scar.

13.

THE STAGES OF GRIEF

I hesitate to write this chapter. I do so because there is a danger in trying to describe reactions to grief or any other experience in neat, well defined steps. No one reacts the same as any other person. Grief is as unique as a finger print. No one reacts in the same pattern. You may go from stage one to stage five and then go to stage three. Or you may be in stage five this morning and them be in stage one before noon.

It is more important to know there are stages than to know how many stages there are or what order they usually take. The stages have been written in various forms and varying numbers. I have found them expressed in three major steps. I have also found them presented as ten steps. Three steps or ten, there does seem to be some very natural stages we go through in our recovery from grief. These are not well-defined steps which identify themselves as you pass. They are generalized patterns of growth you will experience often without recognizing them at all.

The first stage is the period of shock. Your body has a built-in protective device that takes over in tragedy. Everything goes into a state of unreality. It is like a bad dream you seem to be walking through and are expecting to go away before long. You still function, but it is all unreal. You cry and yet do not feel the brokenness is real. You go through the days before the funeral almost in trance. You try to avoid facing the reality for fear the dream will become real, and the numbness will go away.

The second stage is reality. Gradually the numbness wears away, and reality begins to set in. This usually happens after the friends and family are gone, and you are beginning the slow process of having to face the loneliness. The reality stage is the toughest. During this stage you go through times of deep depression and despair. You may feel as if nothing can help, nothing can give the strength to face the days ahead.

During this period of reality you may find yourself becoming almost totally dependent on others. A friend may get calls from you at all hours of the night. Your children may be called upon to hear your cries and moans until you are sure they are disgusted with your weakness.

You may hate yourself for being so dependent, but seem to not know what else to do. You may feel you must talk to someone, then find you have nothing to say except that you hurt and feel as if you cannot make it.

This stage will also pass—believe it or not, it does. The passage is gradual. So gradual you may not notice it passing. You feel a little stronger and call on others a little less. You make a decision, or even meet a crisis, and solve it before you think about calling someone. After this decision is made or crisis is met, it dawns on you that you faced it, and did so on your own. This gives a little more strength and a little more confidence. You are not ready to run and not be weary, but at least you are walking and that is something.

The next stage must be called the reaction stage. You may be in this stage at the same time you are in one of the other stages, for it is not well-defined. Reactions come, and they are normal. No one can list all of the reactions, for they vary with each individual. I can list a few which you may experience, but the list is in no way complete.

You may react with guilt. This is when the "If only I had" hits with a vengeance. During this stage you may feel the need to persecute yourself with guilt, either real or imagined. No amount of arguing can change your mind or your feelings. You feel guilty because right now you need to feel guilty. This is a reaction and it, too, will pass. You will gradually realize you are heaping guilt on yourself because you need to blame somebody, and then you can deal with the feelings more realistically.

You may react with anger. Sometimes it may be irrational anger. You may get mad at that ones who mean the most to you. You may get angry at the one who has died. I have sat with widows who, after much struggle could tell me their feelings. They say, "I pace the floor calling his name and saying, 'How could you leave me like this?'" Though this reaction may seem totally irrational it is not irrational at all. Your feelings are turned upside down and they must land somewhere. They often land in anger at the one who has gone.

Maybe anger is the wrong word. We think of anger in terms of getting mad. Anger can be hurt, frustration, fear, helplessness, or many other feelings. All of these come from the same emotion as anger. When they are stirred up they express themselves any way they can. The guilt reaction is actually anger turned on yourself. Some folks turn it on

71

themselves. Others turn it outward. Most all of us react in anger and must find somewhere for it to land. Anger does not float well. It needs a place to focus.

This too, is a stage that will pass. The best thing to do with these reactions is to recognize their presence and admit they are there. Then the most important thing to understand is that the anger needs to be expressed. Swallowed anger leads to depression. "I fell guilty" or "I feel angry" are both very healthy statements.

The fourth stage is reconstruction. Thank goodness there is another stage. After walking through the stages already mentioned, we come to the reconstruction stage. When this book first appeared I called this stage the recovery stage, but there really is no recovery. We don't "get well." We turn the corner in the way we cope and decide to live again. You may get up to that point many times before you actually turn the corner, but the day will come when things seem to be different and you can face things you have been avoiding and begin to reconstruct your life only this time your life includes a large chunk bitten out of your heart.

The stages also produce symptoms. Again, there is no actual list of all of the possible symptoms. I am listing five of them just to give you an idea about what kind of symptoms there are. Yours may be different from all five of these. All I am trying to say by this list is you will react to your grief. That reaction will be normal for you, and the symptoms of that reaction should be simply accepted as your way of walking through the grief journey. Some of the symptoms are:

Sleep: You may want to sleep all of the time and never seem to get enough. Anyone can see this is an effort to avoid facing the pain of grief, but that may be your natural method of dealing with problems. Some people have a natural tendency to avoid problems. Your way of dealing with a problem may be to ignore it until it goes away. Who is to say your way is wrong? If it works for you, it must be all right. You may react to grief by going to bed and hoping the world goes away. In time, you will be ready to wake up and begin facing your grief, but you must do so when you are ready, not when someone else thinks you should.

Activity: Other folks try to solve problems by staying too busy to notice or to think. You may feel the need for constant motion. Traveling, volunteering for as many tasks as possible, cleaning the house, or just running around in circles—anything to keep from getting still and having to think or feel. That too is a way of avoiding and it will only work for a little while. In time, you too will get off of the treadmill and begin the grief journey.

Hyper-Religious: Some folks find their comfort or their avoidance by becoming almost fanatically religious. You may find yourself searching for as many emotional religious experiences as you can find. Bible studies, prayer meetings, or any type of religious activity seems to fit some desperate need. Your emotions are whirling and seeking any outlet they can find. Religion can furnish a good outlet for these emotions for some people. The one thing to watch out for is pressure to be well before you are well.

Physical Illness: This seems to be especially prevalent among those who cannot feel free to express their grief. You may act very brave and hold up remarkably well. You may enjoy the admiration which comes as people marvel at your strength and courage. You can become trapped in a prison of silence with no way to express your grief. Swallowed grief can lead to illnesses of all or any kinds. Physical illness becomes the perfect way out. We can suffer over the illness and still keep up the front of being strong and courageous over our loss.

Promiscuity: Some will feel such a need to be loved they react in panic. You may go through this period by engaging in activities you would not think of doing under any other circumstances.

All of these symptoms are efforts to avoid facing grief. What is more natural than tying to avoid the unpleasant? All of these symptoms reflect the person's natural method of facing problems. Nothing could be more normal that this.

You must be allowed the time to go through the stages and the freedom to experience the symptoms. There are no short cuts except the short cut of acting well long before you are really well. This short cut leads to more hurt in the long run.

It is far better to understand the natural process of grief recovery and the natural reactions or symptoms caused by the process and then let yourself go through them naturally. Naturally means at your own pace and with your own reactions.

I have a thought or a feeling.
I decide the thought or feeling
is wrong.
Then I decide I should not have
such thoughts or feelings.
I must be crazy, or I would
not have them.
Therefore, I am crazy.
The result is that I feel bad
because I feel bad.

14.

FEELING BAD BECAUSE YOU FEEL BAD

She came to my office to talk about a religious problem. She was convinced she no longer had any faith. She hated church, did not feel as if prayer did any good, was envious of people who seemed to have it all together, and seemed to be plagued with what she called "bad thoughts."

It was almost an hour before she slowed the conversation down enough for me to ask any questions. During this hour she outlined enough sins to ruin all of the saints in heaven. She was a terrible person in her own mind. She had thought of herself as being a very religious person and then everything just fell apart after her husband died.

After he died she felt pressure to carry on with bravery and faith. She enjoyed the people remarking about how strong she was. Going back to church alone was one of the hardest things she had ever done, but she did it. She was ready to tell anyone how her faith had conquered her grief, and she had the victory. Even while she was speaking of victory her insides were screaming, "Not so." She tried to dismiss those thoughts and cover her feelings.

Gradually she could not cover any more. The feelings inside were going to be heard no matter how much she fought to stifle them. She finally had to get honest with herself and face the reality of what she was feeling. Unfortunately, she could not accept the feelings as normal. She thought a person of faith never had bad feelings or bad thoughts.

She felt envious of other couples and told herself that jealousy was a sin.

She thought of herself and her problems and told herself she was selfish and that was wrong.

She tried to pray, could not do so, and told herself she had lost God.

She thought of sex and reacted with horror.

She was tempted to drink and was frightened by the temptation.

All of these feelings she hid. She tried to hide them from herself and then when she could do so no longer, she was determined to hide them from everyone else. She redoubled her efforts to appear well and happy.

Her particular religion seemed to put a great deal of pressure upon her. It seemed to say, "If you pray and read the Bible, you will have no problems." The more she prayed and read the Bible, the worse she felt. This lead to even more feelings of guilt and unworthiness because it seemed to work for others and did not work for her.

Her faith talked a great deal about victory. The meetings she attended were all designed for folks to share the victories in their lives. She felt none.

Depression is caused by swallowed feelings. Anger is the feeling we swallow most often. The anger may express itself as hurt, frustration, disappointment, or self doubt. She swallowed them all and became deeply depressed. Even the depression made her feel guilty. After all, a person of faith is not supposed to feel depressed. Her conclusion was that she had a religious problem. Her conclusion was that she was a bad person.

She was in what I call *The Feel Bad Because You Feel Bad Syndrome*. This syndrome is caused by our having natural feelings and not knowing they are natural. You then reacting by telling yourself you should not feel this way. The next step is to think there is something wrong with you or you would not feel this way. This can have a snowball effect that leads to the conclusion that you must be bad, weak, or crazy, or you would not feel this way. This lady's conclusion centered on her religion. Others can center on the idea of being mentally ill, or that of being weak or just a bad person.

I dealt with her by asking again and again how she was supposed to feel. When she would list for me all of the bad feelings and thought, I would just ask again, "How are you suppose to feel when your husband dies?" I explained to her that grief is a deep wound that needs time to heal and will not just go away, no matter how much religion she had. I said, "If you broke your leg, would you think it weak or nonreligious to be hurt until the leg healed? If not why is it weak or nonreligious to hurt until grief heals?"

At first she protested, "But other people don't think like this."

I said, "At least they do not let you know they think like this."

She looked at me in utter disbelief. To her, I was attacking her religion.

Too often, religion only tells one side of the story. We share the victories with great gusto, but we rarely even talk about the defeats. One of the best things I have done in church was to have a testimony time when we shared our prayer defeats. Some of the very finest Christians stood to express fear and frustration for the first time in their lives. We all sat together and felt normal.

The "Victory Only" approach leaves us convinced everyone has much more faith than we do. It leaves us feeling as though we are the only ones who ever feel the way we feel or the only ones to ever think the thoughts we think. The truth is there are no super people. Most of us are about alike. Everyone has bad thoughts, angers, temptations, fears, and frustrations. If we could be honest with one another, we could feel normal. Since we cannot seem to be this honest, we feel everyone else is a super-religious person and we are spiritual peons.

This is also true outside of religion. Everyone else seems to have it all together while we feel the fears, angers, temptations, and frustrations of living. The longer I live the more convinced I am that underneath the façade we are all just human beings. We just don't let our humanness show.

When grief comes, feelings you never dreamed you had suddenly show up. Since we all play the game of never showing true feelings, we have no idea how others feel. Therefore, you do not really know how others feel. Since you do not know, it is easy to assume your feelings are odd or not proper. You can then decide that since you are thinking or feeling wrong there must be something wrong with you. The result is that you feel bad because you feel bad.

How are you supposed to feel in grief? What kinds of feelings are normal? What is okay, and what is not okay? Maybe it is time for us to get honest.

You are going to be selfish. Selfish is not the right word to use, but it is the word you will probably use to describe your situation. It will feel like selfishness. During grief you will think of yourself almost all of the time. Everything will be related to you. You may even resent anyone talking about someone else's problems. Inside you may cry out, "How dare you tell me of someone else's problem when I am hurting."

If a person tells you how bad he or she feels because they do not know what to say, your reaction might be, "Here I am hurting, and all you can do is tell me how bad you feel—big deal."

These feelings are normal. This is how you should feel. There is no need to go off somewhere and kick yourself for being selfish.

This turning inward to your own needs is not selfishness—it is survival. When you are attacked your whole being goes to survival mode. This is a built-in defense mechanism. It is as natural as craving food when you are hungry. No one ever calls normal eating selfish. Eating is survival. Eating is necessary to staying alive.

Turning to your own needs in grief is also survival. It is also necessary to staying alive. When you have a headache, nothing else matters very much except the ache in your head, you cannot read, you cannot listen to others. You cannot be very concerned about the hurts of others. Headaches dominate while they are there. Heartaches do the same. During the grief journey your whole system is trying to survive and recover. While this is going on you will be dominated by your own hurts and your own needs. Call this selfish if you want to—in reality it is simply surviving to live another day.

You may be envious. How else could you feel if you have lost a mate and other couples seem to be so happy together? You must adjust to loneliness while they seem to flaunt their togetherness.

How else could you feel if your child has died and you see happy family groups enjoying life together? How could you be expected to be joyous at a wedding your child can never have? You are glad for the young couple and the family, but your insides will be aching.

The old statement, "I felt sorry because I had no shoes until I met a man who had no feet" sounds great but frankly, in the middle of winter, I still want some shoes.

You can tell yourself a thousand times how wrong it is to be envious after a loss, but telling yourself won't make it go away. In time it will be less intense, but every happy event will bring it back to mind.

You will probably think of sex. This, of course, will depend on your own feelings and perhaps your age. There is no switch inside you that can be flipped to shut off the natural need for love, affection, and sex. Since God did not provide such a switch, He must understand that these feelings will be there, and you will think about them.

The need for love is as natural as the need for food. When this need is no longer being met, you cry out for it like crying for food when you are starving. Add to this the fact that every emotion you have has been turned upside down by the trauma of grief, and you can begin to see why these feelings and needs are intensified during this time. Again you are in survival mode. During survival all needs become big needs. This need is no exception.

So you may well be selfish, angry, envious, and tempted. Does this mean you are bad, or does it mean you are normal?

The answer is normal. You can face the thoughts and feelings and accept them as a normal part of grief. If you can accept them in this way, you can live with them and live through them. The feelings are bad enough without adding the tension and fear of non acceptance.

If you do not accept these feelings and thoughts as normal you go to war with yourself. Energy needed for recovery is spent on self-hate. At the time you need the most support, you are not giving support to yourself. At the time you need every good word you can get you are receiving bad words from yourself.

The result is that depression is deepened, fears are formed into guilt, and you become a bundle of self-hate.

To not accept these feelings as normal is to invite yourself into the miserable world of feeling bad because you feel bad.

I could try to be the super seller of positive thinking and tell you the changes you face are a glorious opportunity to spread your wings and fly uncharted skies, but I won't.

The changes can produce growth, but not without pain.

The changes will be uncharted, and therefore, scary.

The changes can lead to a new life, only if you allow them to do so.

I cannot change the changes—neither can you.

I cannot lessen the trauma of a single one of them.

I can pull back the curtain and let a little bit of light in so you can see the changes, and the reasons for the changes, and maybe even a way or two to face them with more comfort.

Maybe even give some courage to face them.

At least it will help to know what to expect and why...

Changes are hard enough—unexpected ones are harder.

Misunderstood ones are harder still—

Let's look and try to understand...

SECTION IV

CHANGES

I wonder—
   Does God gossip?
Does He talk to other folks
      about me?
If not, why do they think they
      know His way for me?
If He does
      I wish he would quit it.

15.

THE SEARCH FOR APPROPRIATE BEHAVIOR

The underlying struggle in every grief group I have led is the search for proper behavior. The unasked and unanswered question lurking behind the scenes is "How am I supposed to act now?" No one in any of the groups has ever verbalized the question. It may be no one has known what the question is.

The question gets asked in strange ways. As a matter of fact, it is revealed in statements made far more often than in questions asked.

Someone says, "If I date, everyone in town will talk."

Someone else says, "I would not buy a car for a year because I could just hear them say, 'He is not even cold, and there she is out blowing his money.'"

Another will chime in, "I know I am getting a bad reputation because I go out all of the time. I can just see my neighbors watching me leave again and talking their heads off."

It begins to sound like a group of paranoids getting together to discuss how many people are watching them. In reality it *is* a group of paranoids getting together since everyone in grief has some feelings of paranoia.

The cause of these feelings of paranoia is that no one has defined appropriate behavior for the suddenly single person.

How is a widow to react? How long should she be in mourning? How long before she goes out socially?

How long must she wait before dating? How should she act in a crowd? How does she keep wives from thinking she is after their husbands? Who knows the answer to all of these questions?

How is a widower to act? Who can he call for companionship? The widower is rare in our society because most wives outlive husbands, so there are not many widowers for him to turn to. Can he turn to widows without starting the gossip mills turning? Can he have the relationship of a friend without it looking like the relationship of a lover? Who knows the answer?

The only definition we have ever had for appropriate behavior is an unwritten one. Our culture has imposed some vague, so-called rules upon us, and we seldom question their validity.

One of these unwritten rules is: a widow must wait one year to show respect to her departed husband. Who says it must be one year? What is sacred or respectful about a year? It may take a year or longer before some people want to begin new relationships. If so, fine. There are no rules. God has never written—nor even hinted at—some appropriate length of time for proper mourning.

It may show more respect to the departed mate if you do *not* wait a year. It might say the marriage was good, and I want to experience this kind of good relationship again.

I have told my wife in jest and in seriousness that I want her to marry again as soon as she feels ready and meets the right man. I feel no sense of her needing to wait so everyone will know how much I am missed. I have told her she has made marriage wonderful enough for me that I do not intend to live alone. To me, I would be complimenting her if I chose to go back into a marriage.

Apart from marriage, how about just forming relationships? Won't people talk if enough time has not passed? Yes, some will talk. Some will talk no matter how much time has passed. You cannot live your life in fear of people talking and ever be free to live. You may just have to let them talk.

There are two kinds of pressures placed on a widow or widower.

There is the presumed pressure. Since what is appropriate has never been defined, you may tend to presume how everyone feels about this area. Since you are cut adrift with no guidelines, you tend to feel paranoid as you struggle through in blindness. It is very easy to decide people are talking when in fact they may not be doing so at all. It is very easy to become super-sensitive to everything that is said and to read into statements what is not meant.

It is easy to assume the whole world is watching you to see if you conform to their rules, when in fact few are watching and few have rules. Most folks want you to be happy. A few do not understand. The few will not understand no matter what you do or how you behave. Thank God they are few, and go on.

It becomes necessary to check yourself periodically to see if the pressure is real or presumed. When you feel the pressure mounting, stop to find out where it is coming from. Ask yourself if you are being pressured by real or presumed things. Ask yourself how you know people feel the way you think they feel. There will be enough real pressure without adding presumed pressure to the pile.

But then there is real pressure. There will be those who will "know" exactly how you should feel and act. Unfortunately, they will also tell you. There are enough insensitive and dominating people in this world so everyone will know one or two.

When you are grieving they will be very quick to tell you how weak and silly you are. Their idea is if you sympathize with people, they will never get better. Their creed is: sympathy is bad—it only makes the person worse. They will tell you to buck up.

Then, when you buck up, they will move in with the guilt pumps to be sure you do not buck up too far. They will hint, or even say, you must not have loved very deeply to have forgotten so soon.

These people put you in a double bind. If you grieve too long you are weak. If you don't grieve long enough, you did not love. In neither case will they explain how long "long" is.

The fear of such people can put you in a trap which is difficult to escape. They seem to be always present so you can't avoid them, and you do not want them to think badly of you. So you try to avoid them and cannot seem to do so. You would like to tell them to hush but fear the consequences, so you sit there in the pressure.

To make matters even worse, often these people will be family. How in the world do you tell family to go away?

One of the great freeing experiences of my life was when I finally learned some lessons about me and others. I was in a profession which is constantly criticized. A minister never pleases everyone. Some of the time I felt I never pleased anyone. Everyone "knew" how I should talk, dress, think, smell, and do my job. None of these opinions were the same, so I was bound to be displeasing someone all of the time. I was also bound to hear about it most of the time.

Someone asked me once how I manage to take the criticism I receive. They thought I would tell them how to grow a thick skin. They thought I would tell them some secret formula for not letting criticism get through to bother me. They were wrong. I have never been able to grow skin thick enough. I have no formula for not letting it bother me. Criticism hurts, and it will always hurt. I wish I could tell you that I pray and God speaks, and I no longer feel hurt. I cannot tell you a formula for making it not hurt. I can tell you some things that help me cope with the hurt.

First: I try not to let presumed pressure get to me. I did let it get to me in my early life. I just knew I was being watched constantly and judged unmercifully. I finally discovered I was presuming everyone was like the few. Believe me, they are not. Someone said, "You would be surprised at how many people are not talking about you."

Second: I discovered a basic human right I had missed—the right to determine how bad I am to feel about anything that relates to me.

When you make a mistake there are always people ready to play *blemish*. *Blemish* is the game of pointing out mistakes and telling how bad the mistake is and what the consequences of the mistake are. It goes something like, "That was a dumb thing to do—you have ruined your life and the lives of generations to come."

If you are wrong, there is always someone handy to tell you how wrong and what you must do to correct the wrong.

I once had longer hair than I have now. I had it longer because I was speaking on college campuses, and it helped me relate to that generation. I met a preacher who had a distaste for long hair. He immediately set upon me to let me know how wrong I was and what I must do to correct the wrong. The conversation went like this:

I asked "Whose head is this hair on?"

"Yours."

"If God does not like it, who is he likely to talk to about it—me or you?"

"Why you, I guess."

"If He talks to me, and I do not listen, who is in trouble?"

"Why, you are."

"Then I assume it is my business, isn't it?"

My point is, God does not gossip. If He wants you straightened out, He will talk to you, not to someone else. He does not talk to them about you—He talks to you about you.

This means you have the right and the responsibility to determine right and wrong for yourself. Don't let others force it upon you.

There was a man in a church I served who felt it his duty to straighten me out on several occasions during my time there. One Sunday morning he accosted me with, "That sermon is the worst thing I have ever heard. You have mixed everyone up, and we will never be the same."

I calmly said, "I did what I thought was right. If I made a mistake it is my mistake, and that is as bad as I am going to feel about it."

He began again to explain how bad my mistake was and made sure I knew how bad I should feel.

I interrupted him with, "You did not hear me—if I made a mistake, it is my mistake, and that is as bad as I am going to feel."

He began again.

I interrupted again.

When *he* could not determine how bad I was to feel, there was nothing left to say.

You have the same right. You may have to use the same tactics. You do not have to be mean nor smart aleck, but you do have to be firm. I know you fear standing up to people because you think they will not like you. They probably will like you more after they recover from the shock.

When they lay the guilt on you, just simply say again and again, "I must determine how my life is to go. If I am making a mistake, it is my mistake, and that is as bad as I am going to feel about it."

It is amazing how folks hush when they can no longer determine the course of your life.

Third: I have decided I have two people to please. I cannot please everyone all of the time. I cannot please some any of the time. So I decided whom I should please. My choices are:

I am going to please God as I understand Him. I shall not try to please Him as others understand Him. I shall find His way for me to the best of my ability and follow it. His way for me is too important for me to follow someone else's interpretation.

I am going to please me. I matter. This may sound selfish, but it is actually quite healthy. I must assume the responsibility for myself. I must assume responsibility for my happiness, my actions, my health, and who I am. I cannot do so if I allow others to determine how I am to feel and act and think and be.

What is appropriate behavior? No one knows. No one knows the answer to this question even in general terms. They certainly do not know the answer in the specific terms of you.

You should go out when you are ready.

You should date when you feel it appropriate.

You should have relationships when you need them.

You should spend money when you think it right.

You should just be you.

And if they talk—let 'em talk.

*There is no discomfort
in this world as bad as
Watching a friend hurt and
having no answer.*

16.

THE SEARCH FOR APPROPRIATE FRIENDS

The first question in the grief seminars is, "What is appropriate behavior?" The second is, "What happened to my friends?"

Before death came you had a group of couples, the relationships seemed to be close. When death came they rallied to your side and were absolutely wonderful. During the early days of grief they made promises to stay by your side and help you through your grief. One by one they seemed to drop out of sight.

The ones you counted on the most were probably the first to go. A barrier seemed to develop almost overnight. At first they had plausible reasons for not having been by to see you. Then they seemed to feel guilt and apologized the whole time you were around them. Gradually the relationships were gone.

The old group plans a party, and you are not invited. When you are with them there seems to be very little to talk about. The tension seems to be like a fog hovering over the whole scene.

After a while you begin to feel like the proverbial fifth wheel at every gathering. The only time you are invited is when a couple has a single person they can invite, and they play matchmaker for the two of you.

You will resent their intrusion into your life. You will resent the implication that you are not capable of meeting your own single friends. You might not be capable of meeting single friends, but you do not care to have this broadcast to the whole world.

The usual experience is that many friends—no matter how close before death came—will not remain close after death.

There are exceptions to this, of course. If you are experiencing an exception, count your lucky stars and enjoy your friends. They are rare indeed.

Some exceptions will happen just because of the age group in which you happen to be. If very young, you may still have unmarried friends. If you are older, many of your friends will have already lost a mate, and you will fit right into their life styles.

Most will have to face the loss of friends. Our society is a "couple" world. Everything is geared for couples, from church socials to a night at the opera—everything seems to be designed with couples in mind. Suddenly you are a single in a couple world.

If your loss was a child instead of a mate the loss of friends may still be your experience. Friends will not know how to relate to your loss. They will feel uncomfortable around you. They will feel the tension of not knowing what to say, whether or not to mention your child, and whether or not to talk about the loss. They will have no idea how you feel, and therefore, will be at a loss for words. This tension can easily cause them to avoid you, and thereby, avoid facing the tension.

All of this can cause you to become lonely and bitter. You will find other friends. Most of these new friends will be in the same condition as you are. They will understand because they are there, also. You will often wonder if you are good for one another since there will be times when all you do is get together and cry. It will seem as if you are just prolonging one another's grief.

New friends or not, you will miss the old ones and wonder what happened to the relationships. This wondering can cause you to doubt your own self-esteem. It can cause you to wonder what you did wrong. It can cause you to wonder if they ever really loved you. The result can be a new attack of the "feel bad because you feel bad" syndrome.

The truth is that you did nothing wrong. The truth is that they did love you. There are reasons for this change in relationships—reasons you need to understand. Understanding will not bring the friends back, but it may help you see their perspective and not grow bitter. Let's try to understand what goes on.

First: People do not understand grief. A Midwestern newspaper ran a man-on-the-street survey which asked people how long they thought it took to mourn the loss of a loved one. The answers varied from forty-eight hours to two weeks. Clinical test reveal it takes from eighteen months to two years. About the only people who know how long grief may last are those who have experienced grief themselves. As a society we have been almost without knowledge about grief. No one has told us what it feels like, nor how long it lasts.

The result is your friends will have almost no knowledge about grief. They are in the dark and feel it. When your grief extends beyond a few weeks, they begin to think you should be well by this time. When you do not get well, they begin to think you are odd in some way.

Your options are to try to pretend you are well long before you are, or go on in your grief and let them be uncomfortable. I hope you will not pretend. The more a mourner must live a life of pretense, the more difficult it is to adapt to the normal functions of living.

The first reason, then, is your friends simply do not understand the grief process. I hope this will change. Much is being written in this area. Seminars are being held, studies made. Hopefully, our ignorance will soon pass. It might be a good idea to let your close friends read this book. Perhaps it will help them understand where you are.

Second: Some folks have trouble with intimacy. You can be close friends with another for years and never be intimate. Intimacy is the sharing of feelings. Friends usually get together and share ideas. Rarely do they get together and share feelings. Some people just can not be around feelings. They are not only uncomfortable with yours, they are uncomfortable with their own. If their mate cries, they try to change the subject or leave the room. Now you are feeling, and it shows. They do not know how to deal with the intensity of such feelings, so they run.

Before you get too harsh with your friends, try to remember how you felt before your experience. You probably felt the same sense of discomfort and frustration. You probably avoided the situation of a friend grieving the same way your friends are avoiding you.

Third: We are a "tell" society. We have never discovered the power of the ear. When someone tells us his/her problems we think we must have an answer. If we have no answer, we feel as though we have been no help at all. The frustration of having no answer can cause us to either give shallow answers or just run from the question.

The ear is the most powerful part of the human body. People are healed by the laying on of ears. When you talk out feelings, other feelings change.

Have you ever been angry and tried to tell someone about why you were angry. While you were talking you could not seem to make the incident seem as bad as it was. Finally, you just gave up and said, "Well, I don't know why that made me so mad." This is the power of the ear bleeding off anger.

In grief you need ears. Your friends do not understand this need. They think you are asking for some answer to the whole problem of grief. They do not know any answer because there is no answer. Grief has to be lived through—it cannot be just answered.

You can help your friends in this situation. Tell them you need someone with whom to talk. Tell them at the beginning of the conversation you do not expect an answer and hope they can be comfortable in not having one to give. As you talk, try not to put your conversation together with questions. Instead of saying, "Why did this have to happen?" say, "I am often at a loss to understand why this happened." This is closer to how you feel and does not put your listeners on the spot to come up with an explanation.

If they try to give some answers, with care and kindness tell them, "Thank you, but please understand you do not need to feel on the spot. I am not looking for answers—I am looking for an ear." Tell them it helps just to talk about it with no answers expected or even desired. When you finish talking tell them how much help you have received from the session together. Assure them they have done all you needed.

You may be amazed at how relieved they will be. You may also be amazed at how anxious they will be for you to return for more talk. I am convinced the major problem with friends in grief is right here. They feel like they must have an answer to give you, and they do not have one. The result is that they feel helpless to help, and run from the encounter. You can help them help you. Tell them you need to just borrow their ears, and then let them know how much the loan helped.

You will make new friends. Gradually you will discover you are also uncomfortable with some of the old friends. There may be too many memories there. There may be too much of a contrast between their situations and yours. You may not have as much in common with some friends now as you once had.

Your new friends will be found among those who are experiencing the same trauma as you. These will be lifesavers. You may feel at times that you just reinforce each other's recovery.

Recovery takes a lot of crying. It is good to have someone with whom to cry. After some of these times together you will feel worse. After some of them you will be depressed. Gradually the depression will pass, and you will find you both have grown.

Recovery takes a lot of talking. Folks who never have been there may get tired of talking about it. Folks who have been there understand the need to talk. They will not get tired of being talked to nor of talking.

Recovery takes people. In grief, people need people. If you are to recover, you must force yourself out to where people are. If you lock yourself in and become a hermit, you will never recover.

In almost every town there are singles groups.

In many towns there are grief groups and grief seminars.

If there are none in your town, try to get one started.

The best thing you can have right now is a group of people who understand and give you time to grieve.

If this group is your old group of friends—wonderful.

If not, find some new ones. You need them—and they need you.

"Feel what you feel" is the best advice I can give.

17.

THE SEARCH FOR APPROPRIATE REACTIONS

How should you react if you lose a mate and are at least a little relieved by the loss? The marriage was never right; life together was hard; the marriage became an agreement instead of a relationship. When it was over there was grief, but also relief.

Some folks will feel this way. There is nothing wrong with feeling a sense of relief. The only danger is being unable to accept this feeling as being right or normal. If the feelings cannot be accepted as right and normal, then there will be a great deal of guilt involved. The result may bring forth an effort to make it up to the person who had died.

The "making it up to" can lead to your seeing the one you have lost as larger than life. You forget all flaws, bury all bad memories, and make the person into a saint. You picture the marriage as perfect. You remember your life together as ideal. You will enjoy long conversations about the dear departed.

A few chapters back I said "Feel what you feel." That might be the best advice I can offer. If you feel relieved, then feel it and go on with the business of living.

What happens if the opposite is true? Your marriage was great, and you feel total emptiness now that your mate is gone. This feeling may be more prevalent in women than men. Many women go through an identity crisis after the death of a husband. Most of their lives have been lived as Mrs. John Brown instead of Mary Brown. Gradually their whole identities become meshed in the lives of their husbands. When the husbands are gone, so are the identities.

This is a tough one. You must forge a new identity in the midst of all of the pressures of grief and the struggle for appropriate behavior. You will feel you do not know who you are, how you are to live, and what you are to do.

It becomes necessary to begin all over in the process of living. It is almost like being eighteen years of age again and struggling to find yourself. A great deal of time must be spent in sorting through feelings to discover how you feel about life. How do you want to live? That does not sound profound, but by meshing your life into his, you have not faced up to what you want life to be. "What kind of person do I want to be?" becomes a big question.

A great deal of time must be spent in deciding what kind of life you prefer socially. Your social life has been determined by the preference of your mate. You simply floated into a social style without much thought given to how you wanted the style to be. If your mate was active socially, you were active socially.

Now you are faced with determining what social style fits you. This is the first time you have been called upon to make this kind of choice. You may find yourself wanting a brand new style for a little while. If you have been a home body, you may now go out too much. You may feel an intense desire to catch up on all you have missed. Go ahead. Gradually the pendulum will swing back toward the center.

One problem you can expect is your children may feel threatened by any change in you. They, too, are in grief. They will feel a great need for everything to remain as it was. They will expect the home to be the same. All of the traditions the family has built around Christmas, New Year's, anniversaries, and vacation will become almost sacred to them.

The first holiday after a death can be a disaster. You may not feel ready for such an event. You may dread the thought of preparing meals and trying to carry on as in years past. While you feel this, you will have no idea how to tell the children without hurting their feelings.

The children may begin to hint about how much you have changed. They may even set you down for a talk about your changes and tell you how wrong you are. This attack is not personal. They are reacting to change out of a wish for everything to be as it once was. They have not yet faced the issue of death. Death means things will not be the same as they were.

Be firm. Defend your feelings. At first the children may not be ready to understand or accept. Suggest that they read this book to help them understand and accept the feelings you have, the situation you face, and the changes you must make in your life and lifestyle.

If the first holiday comes and you are not ready, be honest about it. Tell your children how you feel. They may be shocked at first. The shock can be therapeutic. It can help them face the reality of the situation. If they begin to face this reality now, they will be better prepared to face the changes of the future. There may be many such changes to face. You might move. You might change how you live. You might even change with whom you live. Reality at first helps face reality in the future.

SECTION V

THE DAWNING OF A NEW DAY

I have not offered any outlines to follow—
    nor formulas to work—
    nor platitudes to say to yourself.
There are none—
Grief has no short cuts. It is lived through.

If you can grasp the normal—
    avoid the pitfalls—
    and talk it out—
Time will do most of the healing.

I said *most*—not all. For many folks do not become whole
    again. They scab over, but never really heal. They be-
    come defeated by life and never seem to want to live
    again.

Most of these are victims of the pitfalls we have tried to
    avoid.

Some of them just never find the last big step. They wait
    for healing to happen to them. They wait for time to
    take care of it all.

Time does the most in healing—but there must come a
    day when each of us must decide to Live Again—

That day is the one big difference between those who get
    well and those who do not.

May you find this day and let it dawn in your life…

Nothing is as wonderful as suffering in silence. Especially if everyone knows you are doing so.

18.

DO YOU WANT TO GET WELL?

In Biblical days there was a legend about one of the pools in Jerusalem. The growth of the legend is easily explained. The pool evidently gave off a series of air bubbles periodically. Since no one understood the principles of air or bubbles, they gave the phenomenon mystical powers. It was not long until the word passed that whoever was first into the water after the bubbles would be healed.

I am sure there were enough healings over the years to keep the legend alive. We now know much of the illnesses people have are psychosomatic in nature, and, therefore, if some of these people thought they were well, they were well.

I am sure the healings were far enough apart to create a great problem with maintaining hope. A fact even harder on the hope was the ones who were the least ill were able to get into the water first. The chronically ill could never make it in time.

Jesus Christ came to this pool on one occasion. He approached a man who had been lying there trying to be healed for thirty-eight years. He asked the man,

"Do you want to get well?"

The man's answer was very defensive:

"What do you mean, 'Do I want to get well?' I have been here thirty-eight years, but I can't get there first. How can you ask do I want to get well? Of course I do."

The truth is the man may not have really wanted to get well. He probably thought he did. He told himself a thousand times he wanted it. He fantasized about what it would be like. With all of this he still could have not really wanted to get well.

Gradually over the years he may have begun enjoying being a helpless victim. He had no responsibilities to face. He had a ready excuse for any failure. He did not have to work.

There are times when suffering feels so good it is tempting to stay right in the middle of it.

Nothing feels as good as suffering in silence, especially if everyone knows you are. Nothing can be quite as sly as the gradual movement toward enjoying your suffering. You can be there and never know it. You can be there while telling yourself and everyone around you that there is no way on earth you could ever be there. While you shout to the high heavens how much you despise anyone who thrives on sympathy and enjoys suffering, maybe you too must face the "do you want to get well?" bit.

I am not saying this to offend you, nor to frighten you. For goodness sake, don't let it get you into a "feel bad because you feel bad" syndrome. All I am saying is that in most cases there comes a time when you must decide whether or not you want to get well.

Though time is a great healer of grief, even time does not heal automatically. Healing requires both choice and will.

If time alone could heal, and if this healing were automatic, why are there so many people who never get over grief?

I think grief is one of the major social problems of our day. We never think of it as a social problem. We rarely see the connection between grief and the social ills of our time. We have no way of knowing how many alcoholics, divorces, emotional problems and neurotic people began their spiral out of some grief or trauma which they never faced and never resolved.

A friend of mine has great neurotic fears. Most of them are totally unfounded. It is very difficult to understand how a grown man can fear so many things until you discover the background. When he was fifteen years old his father died of suicide while my friend was in the same house. He was the first on the scene. This shock is enough to scar anyone who is fifteen years of age. The event was made much worse by the way the family reacted to this tragedy. They were deeply embarrassed. Their response was to never talk about it.

The young man could not talk to the family and was forbidden to talk to anyone outside the family. He developed a great deal of guilt, blaming the death on things he had done to upset his father. This guilt was totally unfounded, but if guilt cannot be talked about, it cannot go away. He developed fears that he, too, might one day become a suicide. He developed fantasies about how he could have stopped his father. He blamed himself for watching a television show at the time of his father's death.

None of the guilt was dealt with, and, therefore, time, instead of healing, added to the neurotic fears. He drank to avoid thinking about the past. He developed a sense of foreboding about the future. It was as if a great cloud came across his life and would not go away.

Years later he was able to deal with the event and its consequences. He was then faced with the choice of "do you want to get well?"

In all counseling experiences the therapist looks for motivation. If people want to get well, he can help them. If they do not want to, there is nothing he can do. I often say, "People cannot be helped until they want to be helped. Most of the time they do not want to be helped until they hurt."

The hardest part of my job is waiting until people have hurt enough to want to get well. It often looks as though they could not hurt any more, but they still are not ready and must hurt even more. People do not react this way because they are crazy or stubborn. It is just that the pain of getting well must ultimately be less than the pain of staying in their situations.

For example, often the best cure for alcoholics is to withdraw support and let them hit bottom. The hope is that they have a high bottom. A high bottom means they get miserable enough to be motivated before they have ruined everything in their lives.

To these people I say, "I do not accept *I can't*—I only accept *I won't*. As long as you say *I can't*, you will never move. Movement can only happen when you begin to assume responsibility for yourself and say *I won't* instead of *I can't*. You may say *I won't* because of some very good reasons, but to say *I can't* is to play the role of victim."

Now, all of this applies to you and your grief. There must come a time when you assume responsibility for your own recovery. There is no timetable. You will come to it when you are ready. When you get there, your choice is to say

"I want to get well" or to say "I can't." If you say "I can't," growth will stop and wait for your decision to get well.

I have led several groups designed to help people get over grief. I always enjoy the relationship with these people. I always learn a great deal from the relationship. The hardest part of leading the group is the facing up to disbanding the group. If the group is learning and growing, the members usually want to continue. I am softhearted and hate to face the task of weaning people away from the group. The danger in not doing so is that the members will become dependent on the group and never assume responsibility for themselves.

Sometimes one or two members will wean themselves. They come to the point of decision and decide to get well. After the decision to get well, those members no longer feel the need of the group, and they drop out on their own.

The other group members are not so easy to cut loose. They raise the protest of not being ready. They manipulate me. They even try to lay guilt upon me. I must steel myself to realize love is doing what people need—not what they want. If these people are to grow, they must be cut loose to be on their own.

Each group has at least one problem person. This one is usually very vocal with opinions about the hopelessness of the situation. Every suggestion is met with thirteen reasons why it will not work. Anytime someone sounds hopeful of the future, this person shoots them down with pessimism.

I go along with this problem person for quite a few sessions. I know he/she is just not ready to get well. The condition is revealed by the resistance shown at any help offered. I know the day may well come when he/she will want to get well and all of this resistance will change. If resistance persists, I usually arrange to see the person privately. In the private session I let him/her vent feelings for awhile and then confront him/her with the statement, "I am not sure you want to get well."

One lady I confronted in this manner immediately became angry and lashed out at me. After the storm she calmed down and began to face the issue.

Without meaning to, she had been enjoying the suffering. The suffering hurt, but it brought sympathy and attention from friends and family. When the sympathy and attention ceased, she redoubled her efforts at suffering to get it all back.

Without meaning to, she was finding comfort in her suffering. She could blame all of her failures on her hurt. She could lash out at people and then say it was caused by her grief.

She was finding justification in her grief. In a great number of cases a person's lifestyle changes radically after the death of a mate. This woman had changed from the model church-going mother to a lady who seemed to be intent on experiencing all of the fun she missed in life. As long as her grief was there no one could confront her about her behavior. If the grief was gone, she would have to justify the change in behavior to her children and her church.

She looked at me and said, "My grief is still here because I need it, isn't it?"

I said, "Yes, I think so."

She decided it was time to stop hiding behind the grief. She felt she was strong enough to go on without it. She was.

Some people hang on to their grief because they fear that getting better means they are forgetting the person who has died. Some find it hard to move on because they feel closest to their loved one when they are hurting.

A mother I have been companioning has developed a pattern. If she begins to show progress, she will get out her daughter's diary and read until she is in deep pain. She does so in order to feel close and cannot believe that this closeness will not go away if she decides to live again. To her, staying in the pain is the only way to remember and properly honor her daughter.

You may not ever want to keep your grief because you need it. Even so, it is helpful to stop every now and then along the way to examine where you are, and watch out for the trap of wanting to sit down in your grief and park. We all need to ask ourselves, "Do I want to get well?"

Growth is
saying good-bye
AND
saying hello.

19.

SAYING GOOD-BYE AND SAYING HELLO

She never thought her husband would die. Her marriage was only a few years old and blissfully happy. She had been married before, and so had her husband. Both of them came out of bad marriages intent on forming a good one, and they formed a good one. His death was sudden—her recovery was far from sudden. She carried on with a smiling outside and a hurting inside for two years. Everyone assumed she had recovered and was living again. She went through the motions. She also went through the reactions. She tried to drown the hurt in a series of affairs. None of them could satisfy for more than a fleeting moment.

She told me the day came when she had to decide whether to live or die. This decision did not mean thoughts of physical death nor suicide. To die meant she would just wither up in spirit and become a very bitter person. She said the decision came at a very definite time. She remembers what day it was and the time of day it happened. She decided to live again.

Her name is June. She, too, had lost a husband. We are great friends, so we talked for many hours during her grief process. One day I was telling her that often people come to a certain day of decision, and that sometimes there were clues to mark the event. Often there will be some one thing which cannot be faced or discarded. It may be a favorite chair you cannot sit in. It may be clothing you cannot part with. It may be any physical thing.

June immediately said, "The desk! I have not been able to clean out the desk. It has all of the family pictures in it. It has far too many memories around it. He sat there so many nights and did his book work. I rolled down the top, locked the drawers and have not been able to go near it"

I told her there was no hurry. In her own time she would decide to clean it out. When she decided to do so it would probable signal her decision to get well. I urged her not to hurry, not to force the event. Let it happen when it happens.

Late one night June called me to her home. I found her beaming beside a clean desk. Months had passed since our talk, and I had forgotten the details, so it took a moment for the significance to hit me. Her day had come. She had decided to get well.

Your experience may not be like either of these. It may not happen on a given day or at a specific time. It may not be signaled by some physical thing you are ready to face. But a day can come for you just the same.

If it comes as a dramatic event, then you will know it is there and can relate your recovery to that day. If it comes as a quiet event, one day you will notice you feel better and then remember you have felt better for several days. You will remember you have not been depressed for a few days. You will remember you have been laughing more of late. You may not know how or why or when, but you seem to have passed a mark in your pilgrimage.

Growth is saying good-bye and saying hello. All growth is saying good-bye and saying hello. We say good-bye to childhood before we say hello to the adult experience. We say good-bye to petty things before we say hello to major things.

Good-bye does not have to be in anger—it can often be as a good-bye to an old friend. Good-bye does have to be said in hurt. It never is pleasant to say good-bye. It is always most painful to say good-bye in death. No one can prepare you for this good-bye. No one can lessen the hurt. No one can make you want to. Even in the hurt, good-bye can lead to hello. Good-bye can lead to growth.

The Gestalt concept of counseling deals with the good-bye. In this concept every event has the three elements of thought, feeling and memory. As time passes the three elements get isolated from one another. After several years it is possible to have the feelings without the thought or the memory. This type of counseling tries to go back and re-connect the three. It becomes necessary to dig up the past events so the memory is once again vivid. Then an effort must be made to remember the thoughts, the experience created, and the feelings which were felt then. The joining of the three elements explains the feelings. It seems to say, "See, you have feared all of these years—here is where the fear started."

After the three are joined together you say good-bye to them. It sounds simple and easy. It is neither simple nor easy. It takes many such sessions of saying good-bye before the good-bye is final.

I often tell people who are suffering the grief of divorce that there is divorce, and then there is emotional divorce. The emotional divorce comes much later than the actual one. Emotional divorce comes when you are ready to say good-bye and say hello.

All of this applies to you and your grief. The Gestalt idea applies in the sense that if good-byes are not said now, they may have to be said in years to come. The emotional divorce applies in the sense that there is the facing of the loss emotionally.

I repeat—there is no time limit for this event. You will come to it in your own way and at your own time. There is also no set way the experience happens. Your experience will be uniquely yours.

When you are ready to face the emotional loss, the important thing is to give yourself permission to get well. In the first of the book I urged you to give yourself permission to grieve. Now I urge you to give yourself permission to stop grieving.

A strange thing happens to us in grief. We seem to sentence ourselves to a set time for the grief to last. One man said he literally sentenced himself to three years after he lost his wife. He had no idea why he settled on three years—it just seemed to him to be the right number. Until his sentence was up he absolutely rejected any idea of getting out with friends, dating or even having fun. For three years he lived as a recluse. When the term passed, he came out.

Some people sentence themselves for life. Any thought of remarriage or of any other kind of normal life is rejected. They seem to tell themselves they have had their good times, and the good times are now over. The rest of their lives must be spent in loneliness.

The struggle to give yourself permission to get well will not be easy. Social mores and inbred value systems will fight you every step of the way.

Life is not to end with the death of a loved one. You are to grow. You are never supposed to stop growing. You do not know the reasons you have been called to face grief. One thing I am sure of—you were not called upon to do so as punishment. God does not parlay one life against another. He does not take one life to punish another. He took the life He took because He thought it best for that life. Period. To think He took another person's life to teach you a lesson, or to punish you, is arrogance. This says your life is more important than the life of the one He took.

Neither did He take the life to grow you. That, too, is arrogance. Again, He did what was best for the person He came to claim.

It was not done for your growth, but growth can come from the event. This growth can be released much easier if you do not see the death as punishment, or as a sentence to a life of loneliness.

You have new experiences ahead of you. You have new worlds to explore, new feelings to feel, new relationships to grow, and in the process, a new you can result.

This new you will not come easily, nor will it come quickly. You will crawl before you walk. It is like beginning a whole new life all over again. *But it can come*—believe me. It can come.

Give yourself permission to say good-bye. The life you shared may have been marvelous, or it may have been less than pleasant, but now you have learned the lessons of this period of living. The life ahead is uncharted and uncertain, but it is to be lived, and through it you are to grow.

After you say good-bye, then say hello to a new day—wonder what it will be like?

There is one test for whether or not your purpose is done. If you are alive, it is not finished.

20.

PURPOSE

There are two great days in life: the day you were born and the day you discover why you were born. Unfortunately, some people never discover the "why".

Why are you here? What purpose is there to life? This matters if you are coming out of grief. If you see the wrong purpose, you will see very little hope for your future.

Too much of the time we get purpose all messed up with success and vocation. We are here to do something. We are here to do something well and be famous for it. The better we perform, the better we are, and the better we fulfill our purpose.

This idea works fine until we are old and must retire. When the job is gone, so is our value. If our worth gets wrapped up in what we do, when we must stop all sense of worth dies.

I do not believe in reincarnation. I even hope it is not true. There is one concept of reincarnation I wish we could grasp. What if we go through life again and again with the purpose of each trip being what we learn and what we become? The first time through, we learn and become to some level. The next time through we develop further and polish the product even more. What if we had a choice each time as to whether or not we took another whack at it? This time we tried it again to see if we could grasp more insight and become more of a whole person than before.

I do not believe it happens this way. I do believe this pictures the correct idea of purpose. We are here to become. We are valuable because of what we are, not what we do.

If we could grasp this concept, it would change our lives. It could even change our world. Now people have value because of what they have or what they do. I have a friend whose favorite statement is, "I believe the golden rule— them what's got the gold does the ruling." This is the result of purpose being to do or to get.

I once made a list of the five people who have had the greatest influence on my life. I was amazed at the list. No one on the list had ever been "successful". Many of them were very poor. None of them had been well-known. None of them had made any big impact on the world. All of them had influence on me because of who they were instead of what they did.

My father-in-law was the most successful person on the list. His influence had nothing to do with his success. When he became quite ill I went to see him and took my very young granddaughter along for him to see. He was quite depressed about his inability to be up and doing the things he had always done. I told him I had brought my granddaughter to see him because it was important that she know him. I wanted her to grow up knowing him, but I probably would never get around to telling her what he did—I would be too busy telling her who he was.

If purpose is to become, then our task must be to get on with the becoming.

If we suffer loss—we live through it and become.

If we face poverty—we learn the lessons and become.

If we are blessed with riches—we learn to relate to money and become.

If we face the death of a loved one—even this becomes part of our becoming.

You are here to become.

If you have become kind—you are one of the significant people on the earth.

If you have become patient—you have more to share than the richest of men.

If you have become loving—no one is more valuable to our world than you.

Loss has come—Death has come—Trial has come. You and I have walked a ways together. Hopefully the walk has been helpful. Above all else, I hope you grasp the concept of purpose—through it all you are here to become. You become when you live through it all.

Health is saying, "I started with the purpose of becoming a whole human being. Good times have come, storms have come, life has come, life has gone—through it all the purpose is still the same. I must become.

Now, I learn a new lesson, take a new step and move toward the becoming."

About the Author

Doug Manning

Doug's career has included minister, counselor, business executive, author and publisher. He and his wife, Barbara, have been parents to four daughters and long-term caregivers to three parents.

After thirty years in the ministry, Doug began a new career in 1982 and has devoted his time to writing, counseling and leading seminars in the areas of grief and elder care. His publishing company, In-Sight Books, Inc., specializes in books, video and audio productions specifically designed to help people face some of the toughest challenges of life.

Doug's latest efforts have been on the internet as he has become a blogger with his new website dealing with issues in the areas of grief and elder care. The Care Community is a website provided by In-Sight Books, Inc. free of charge to any who wish to join. It is designed to be a resource of help and support for people in grief or involved in caring for an elderly loved one. Read Doug's blogs and respond with your own experiences. Visit www.TheCareCommunity.com.

Doug has a warm, conversational style in which he shares insights from his various experiences. Sitting down to read a book from Doug is like having a long conversation with a good friend.

Selected Resources from In-Sight Books

Books by Doug Manning
Grief
The Special Care Series
Lean On Me Gently: Helping Children Grieve
Thoughts for the Lonely Nights (also available on CD)
Thoughts for the Grieving Christian (also available on CD)
The Funeral: A Chance to Touch, A Chance to Serve, A Chance to Heal
Thoughts for the Holidays: Finding Permission to Grieve
The Power of Presence: Helping People Help People

Elder Care
The Gifts You Bring Series:
Your Gift of Presence
Your Gift of Peace
Your Gift of Participation
Share My Lonesome Valley: The Slow Grief of Long-Term Care
When Love Gets Tough: The Nursing Home Decision

Other Resource from In-Sight Books
I Know Someone Who Died coloring book by Connie Manning
The Empty Chair: The Journey of Grief After Suicide by Beryl Glover
The Shattered Dimension: The Journey of Grief After Suicide Video with Beryl Glover & Glenda Stansbury
Comfort Cards bereavement cards

For a catalog or ordering information:
In-Sight Books, Inc.
800.658.9262 or 405.810.9501
www.InSightBooks.com   OrdersAndInfo@InSightBooks.com

thecarecommunity.com

Visit TheCareCommunity.com for Doug's blogs on Grief and Elder Care